You See It

Renee Jones

Table Of Content

INSPIRATION 6

DETERMINATION 38

COURAGE 70

EXPERIENCE 102

GROWTH 134

Introduction

As you read Speak It Until You See It, I pray that your faith is strengthened, and you allow it to minister to your heart, mind, and soul. Let healing step in and you release all your hurts, pains, and things that has weighed you down.

As you journey through this journal, may your faith, dreams, aspirations, and goals be revived. Each day I want you to affirm those daily affirmations so that you can walk into your true self.

Pull out those pens and let us journey together through the discovery of your true self!

Let's grow together. Transforming our lives one word, one day at a time.

Inspiration

Day 1

I AM BEAUTIFUL AND I AM
NOT DEFINED BY MY FLAWS.

_____

_____

_____

_____

_____

_____

_____

_____

_____

_____

_____

Day 2

I AM UNIQUE AND THERE IS NO ONE CREATED LIKE ME.

_____

_____

_____

_____

_____

_____

_____

_____

_____

_____

_____

Inspiration

Day 3

I WILL SEE MYSELF THE WAY
GOD SEES ME.

_____

_____

_____

_____

_____

_____

_____

_____

_____

_____

Day 4

MY BEAUTY IS NOT FOR EVERYONE, MY
BEAUTY IS FOR THOSE WHO CAN SEE IT.

_____

_____

_____

_____

_____

_____

_____

_____

_____

_____

_____

Day 5

IF I FALL, I WILL GET BACK UP. THERE
IS A WINNER ON THE INSIDE OF ME.

_____

_____

_____

_____

_____

_____

_____

_____

_____

_____

_____

Day 6

I AM A CONQUERER! I HAVE NO FEAR
OF WALKING OUT ON FAITH.

_____

_____

_____

_____

_____

_____

_____

_____

_____

_____

_____

_____

Day 7

IT IS OKAY IF I MAKE A MISTAKE, BUT
IT IS NOT OKAY TO QUIT BECAUSE
OF A MISTAKE.

_____

_____

_____

_____

_____

_____

_____

_____

_____

_____

_____

Day 8

I AM STRONG, PATIENT, AND POLITE.
I AM ALL WOMAN!

_____

_____

_____

_____

_____

_____

_____

_____

_____

_____

_____

Day 9

I WILL NOT CRY OVER SPILLED MILK; I
WILL FIND A CAT TO GIVE IT TO. I
AM A NURTURER.

Day 10

I AM SOMEONES INSPIRATION!
IT IS BIGGER THAN ME.

_____

_____

_____

_____

_____

_____

_____

_____

_____

_____

Day 11

I AM WHAT I THINK ABOUT MYSELF NOT WHAT OTHERS THINK I AM.

_____

_____

_____

_____

_____

_____

_____

_____

_____

_____

_____

Day 12

I AM AMAZING! I AM AMAZING! I AM AMAZING!

_____

_____

_____

_____

_____

_____

_____

_____

_____

_____

_____

Day 13

THE PERSON I SEE IN THE MIRROR IS A BEAUTIFUL BLESSING.

Day 14

I AM WHAT I SAY NOT WHAT
OTHERS SAY I AM.

_____

_____

_____

_____

_____

_____

_____

_____

_____

_____

_____

Day 15

EVERYDAY IS A STRIDE TO MY DESTINY.

Day 16

I AM A SPECIAL CREATION. I
HAVE A PURPOSE!

_____

_____

_____

_____

_____

_____

_____

_____

_____

_____

_____

_____

Day 17

I AM STILL ALIVE BECAUSE I MATTER.

Day 18

MY SCARS ARE PROOF THAT I AM STRONG!

_____

_____

_____

_____

_____

_____

_____

_____

_____

_____

_____

Day 19

MY THOUGHTS HELP ME BE THE BEST VERSION OF MYSELF!

_____

_____

_____

_____

_____

_____

_____

_____

_____

_____

_____

_____

Day 20

I AM MORE THAN MY SURROUNDINGS!

_____

_____

_____

_____

_____

_____

_____

_____

_____

_____

_____

_____

Day 21

I WILL BE WHO I WAS CREATED TO BE
NO MATTER HOW LONG IT TAKES
TO GET THERE.

_____

_____

_____

_____

_____

_____

_____

_____

_____

_____

Day 22

CONSISTENCY IS KEY TO ANYTHING WORTH HAVING.

_____

_____

_____

_____

_____

_____

_____

_____

_____

_____

_____

Day 23

MY SUCCESS IS NOT BASED ON THINGS, IT'S BASED ON ME DOING MY BEST.

_____

_____

_____

_____

_____

_____

_____

_____

_____

_____

Day 24

I AM INSPIRED BY THE FACT
THAT I AM STILL ALIVE.

_____

_____

_____

_____

_____

_____

_____

_____

_____

_____

_____

Day 25

I AM ONE STEP CLOSER TO MY
PURPOSE THAN I WAS YESTERDAY.

Day 26

I AM CREATED FOR GREATNESS AND I
WILL LET GREATNESS TAKE ITS COURSE.

_____

_____

_____

_____

_____

_____

_____

_____

_____

_____

_____

_____

Day 27

YOU CAN DO IT! YOU HAVE BEEN
DOING IT SO FAR, KEEP IT MOVING!

_____

_____

_____

_____

_____

_____

_____

_____

_____

_____

_____

Day 28

THE JOURNEY THAT I TAKE IS TAILORMADE JUST FOR ME!

_____

_____

_____

_____

_____

_____

_____

_____

_____

_____

_____

Day 29

INSPIRATION COMES IN MANY WAYS.
I WILL BE INSPIRED EVERY DAY!

_____

_____

_____

_____

_____

_____

_____

_____

_____

_____

Day 30

GRACE GOT ME HERE AND I AM GOING
TO LET IT CARRY ME THE REST
OF THE WAY!

_____

_____

_____

_____

_____

_____

_____

_____

_____

_____

_____

Day 31

I WILL REMAIN INTACT; I WILL HANDLE
WHAT I CAN AND THE REST I WILL
GIVE TO GOD.

Determination

Today I Am Determined

Day 1

I WILL LOVE WHO I AM CREATED TO BE NO MATTER WHAT!

_____

_____

_____

_____

_____

_____

_____

_____

_____

_____

Day 2

I AM THE LEADER OF MY LIFE
AND I WILL LEAD IT WITH A
DETERMINED MIND.

_____

_____

_____

_____

_____

_____

_____

_____

_____

_____

_____

Today I Am Determined

Day 3

I WILL FIND STRENGTH IN MY
FLAWS. THERE IS GOOD IN ME.

_____

_____

_____

_____

_____

_____

_____

_____

_____

_____

_____

Day 4

I AM DETERMINED TO AVOID ALL
NEGATIVITY TODAY. I WILL FIND
GOOD IN MY SITUATION.

_____

_____

_____

_____

_____

_____

_____

_____

_____

_____

_____

Today I Am Determined

Day 5

I AM DETERMINED NOT TO LET
ANYTHING CAUSE ME TO
LOSE FOCUS TODAY.

Today I Am Determined

Day 6

I WILL CONQUER ANY OBSTACLES
THAT MAY ARISE TODAY.

_____

_____

_____

_____

_____

_____

_____

_____

_____

_____

_____

_____

Day 7

IT IS OKAY NOT TO GET IT RIGHT EVERY
TIME. HOWEVER, IT IS NOT OKAY
NOT TO TRY AGAIN.

Day 8

I AM DETERMINED TO BE GREAT. I WILL
BE SUCCESSFUL ACCORDING TO GODS
PLAN FOR MY LIFE.

_____

_____

_____

_____

_____

_____

_____

_____

_____

_____

_____

Today I Am Determined

Day 9

NO LONGER WILL I FOCUS AND WASTE
TIME ON THINGS OR PEOPLE WHO
DO NOT VALUE ME.

_____

_____

_____

_____

_____

_____

_____

_____

_____

_____

Today I Am Determined

Day 10

I WILL REACH AND MAKE MY
DREAMS A REALITY. SOMEONE IS
DEPENDING ON ME.

_____

_____

_____

_____

_____

_____

_____

_____

_____

_____

_____

_____

Today I Am Determined

Day 11

I AM DETERMINED TO NOT LET
OTHERS DICTATE WHO I AM.

_____

_____

_____

_____

_____

_____

_____

_____

_____

_____

Day 12

I AM DETERMINED
I AM SUCCESSFUL
I AM BEAUTIFUL
I AM WHO GOD SAY I AM!

_____

_____

_____

_____

_____

_____

_____

_____

_____

_____

Day 13

I AM DETERMINED TO BE THE
REFLECTION OF THE BEST
VERSION OF MYSELF.

Day 14

I CONTROL MY MOOD. I AM
DETERMINED TO CONSISTENTLY BE ME.

_____

_____

_____

_____

_____

_____

_____

_____

_____

_____

_____

Day 15

I WILL NOT STOP EVEN IF I STUMBLE;
I WILL SHAKE MYSELF OFF AND
KEEP WALKING.

_____

_____

_____

_____

_____

_____

_____

_____

_____

_____

_____

Today I Am Determined

Day 16

I AM UNIQUE! MY PURPOSE IS MINE
AND I WILL WALK IN IT.

_____

_____

_____

_____

_____

_____

_____

_____

_____

_____

Day 17

I AM DETERMINED TO LIVE AND NOT
JUST EXIST. THE WORLD WAS
CREATED JUST FOR ME.

_____

_____

_____

_____

_____

_____

_____

_____

_____

_____

Today I Am Determined

Day 18

MY STRUGGLE AND HARDSHIPS MADE
ME STRONG. I AM DETERMINED
I WILL NOT GIVE UP.

_____

_____

_____

_____

_____

_____

_____

_____

_____

_____

_____

_____

Today I Am Determined

Day 19

WHAT I THINK ABOUT MYSELF
DETERMINES MY SUCCESS, NOT THE
OPINIONS OF OTHERS.

_____

_____

_____

_____

_____

_____

_____

_____

_____

_____

_____

Today I Am Determined

Day 20

MY REACH WILL SPREAD PAST
MY CURRENT SITUATION.

_____

_____

_____

_____

_____

_____

_____

_____

_____

_____

_____

Today I Am Determined

Day 21

I WILL BE CONSISTENT IN WORKING
ON ME DAILY.

_____

_____

_____

_____

_____

_____

_____

_____

_____

_____

_____

Today I Am Determined

Day 22

BEGINNING WITH THE ENDING RESULTS
IN MIND WILL KEEP ME FOCUSED.

_____

_____

_____

_____

_____

_____

_____

_____

_____

_____

_____

Today I Am Determined

Day 23

I AM DETERMINED TO GIVE MY BEST
IN EVERYTHING I DO.

_____

_____

_____

_____

_____

_____

_____

_____

_____

_____

_____

Today I Am Determined

Day 24

I AM WHERE I AM BECAUSE I AM
DETERMINED NOT TO GIVE UP.

_____

_____

_____

_____

_____

_____

_____

_____

_____

_____

_____

Day 25

RUNNING FAST DOES NOT GUARANTEE
A WIN, CONSISTENCY DOES.

_____

_____

_____

_____

_____

_____

_____

_____

_____

_____

Today I Am Determined

Day 26

WHAT I ACHIEVE IS DETERMINED BY
MY DRIVE TO GET IT DONE.

_____

_____

_____

_____

_____

_____

_____

_____

_____

_____

_____

Today I Am Determined

Day 27

DETERMINATION WILL ALLOW YOU TO
STAY THE COURSE NO MATTER THE
DISTRACTIONS OR OBSTACLES.

_____

_____

_____

_____

_____

_____

_____

_____

_____

_____

Today I Am Determined

Day 28

EVEN WHEN IT GETS TOUGH,
I WILL OVERCOME IT.

_____

_____

_____

_____

_____

_____

_____

_____

_____

_____

Today I Am Determined

Day 29

I WILL EXPECT SOMETHING GOOD OUT
OF EVERY DAY, NO MATTER WHAT
IS GOING ON.

_____

_____

_____

_____

_____

_____

_____

_____

_____

_____

_____

Today I Am Determined

Day 30

I AM DETERMINED TO FOLLOW GRACE
AS MERCY GUIDES ME TO MY
DESTINE PLACE.

_____

_____

_____

_____

_____

_____

_____

_____

_____

_____

_____

Day 31

I WILL REMAIN FOCUSED ON MY
BUSINESS AND CREATING
BETTER FOR ME.

_____

_____

_____

_____

_____

_____

_____

_____

_____

_____

_____

Courage

I Take Courage in Knowing

Day 1

I WILL NO LONGER FEAR THE UNKOWN.

_____

_____

_____

_____

_____

_____

_____

_____

_____

_____

_____

I Take Courage in Knowing

Day 2

I WILL TAKE CHARGE OF MY LIFE NO MATTER WHAT!

_____

_____

_____

_____

_____

_____

_____

_____

_____

_____

_____

I Take Courage in Knowing

Day 3

BEING VULNERABLE MAKES ME STRONG.

_____

_____

_____

_____

_____

_____

_____

_____

_____

_____

Day 4

I WILL FIND THE COURAGE TO WALK
AWAY FROM ANYTHING THAT
CAUSES DISTRACTIONS.

_____

_____

_____

_____

_____

_____

_____

_____

_____

_____

_____

I Take Courage in Knowing

Day 5

I HAVE THE COURAGE TO CHOOSE ME.

_____

_____

_____

_____

_____

_____

_____

_____

_____

_____

I Take Courage in Knowing

Day 6

WITH MY NEW COURAGE
I WILL PERSEVERE.

_____

_____

_____

_____

_____

_____

_____

_____

_____

_____

_____

Day 7

IF IT DOES NOT HAPPEN THE FIRST
TIME, I WILL KEEP TRYING
UNTIL IT DOES.

_____

_____

_____

_____

_____

_____

_____

_____

_____

_____

I Take Courage in Knowing

Day 8

I HAVE THE COURAGE TO BELIEVE I
WILL SUCCEED BEFORE I SEE IT.

_____

_____

_____

_____

_____

_____

_____

_____

_____

_____

_____

_____

Day 9

I HAVE THE COURAGE TO ACCEPT
THAT I CAN NOT CONTROL OR CHANGE
EVERYTHING. AND THE COURAGE
TO KNOW THE DIFFERENCE.

I Take Courage in Knowing

Day 10

I AM ENCOURAGED THAT I AM ONE DAY CLOSER TO ACHIEVING MY DREAMS.

_____

_____

_____

_____

_____

_____

_____

_____

_____

_____

_____

I Take Courage in Knowing

Day 11

I NOW HAVE THE COURAGE TO
SPEAK UP FOR MYSELF.

_____

_____

_____

_____

_____

_____

_____

_____

_____

_____

_____

I Take Courage in Knowing

Day 12

I AM ENCOURAGED! IT IS A NEW DAY! I HAVE ACCOMPLISHED SO MUCH.

_____

_____

_____

_____

_____

_____

_____

_____

_____

_____

I Take Courage in Knowing

Day 13

I TAKE COURAGE IN SEEING THE POSITIVE CHANGES IN MY LIFE.

I Take Courage in Knowing

Day 14

COURAGE IS APPLYING NEW THINGS
TO YOUR LIFE DAILY TO IMPROVE
YOURSELF.

_____

_____

_____

_____

_____

_____

_____

_____

_____

_____

_____

I Take Courage in Knowing

Day 15

I AM GLAD TO KNOW THAT I WAS
CREATED TO BE SPECIAL ON PURPOSE.

I Take Courage in Knowing

Day 16

I AM EXCITED ABOUT THE NEW JOURNEY AND TO SEE NEW THINGS.

_____

_____

_____

_____

_____

_____

_____

_____

_____

_____

_____

Day 17

GIVING UP ISNO LONGER IN MY
THOUGHTS OR VOCABULARY.

_____

_____

_____

_____

_____

_____

_____

_____

_____

_____

_____

I Take Courage in Knowing

Day 18

MY PERSEVERANCE CAUSE ME TO
ENCOURAGE MYSELF IN HARD TIMES.

_____

_____

_____

_____

_____

_____

_____

_____

_____

_____

_____

_____

I Take Courage in Knowing

Day 19

IT'S A GREAT FEELING TO KNOW MY LIFE WILL TOUCH OTHERS.

Day 20

COURAGE IS WITHIN ME; I JUST HAVE TO USE IT.

_____

_____

_____

_____

_____

_____

_____

_____

_____

_____

_____

I Take Courage in Knowing

Day 21

I AM EXCITED ABOUT WHAT'S AHEAD FOR MY LIFE!

_____

_____

_____

_____

_____

_____

_____

_____

_____

_____

_____

I Take Courage in Knowing

Day 22

I HAVE THE COURAGE THAT I WILL NOT
FAIL; FAILURE IS NOT AN OPTION.

_____

_____

_____

_____

_____

_____

_____

_____

_____

_____

_____

I Take Courage in Knowing

Day 23

IT TAKES COURAGE TO KEEP GOING
WHEN THINGS ARE NOT IN YOUR FAVOR.

_____

_____

_____

_____

_____

_____

_____

_____

_____

_____

_____

I Take Courage in Knowing

Day 24

I FIND COURAGE IN THE THINGS I
HAVE GAINED BECAUSE I STAYED
THE COURSE.

_____

_____

_____

_____

_____

_____

_____

_____

_____

_____

_____

Day 25

I TAKE COURAGE IN MY ACHIEVEMENTS BECAUSE I DID IT.

_____

_____

_____

_____

_____

_____

_____

_____

_____

_____

_____

I Take Courage in Knowing

Day 26

PERSEVERANCE CAUSED ME TO EVALUATE MY PROGRESS.

_____

_____

_____

_____

_____

_____

_____

_____

_____

_____

_____

Day 27

I TAKE COURAGE IN KNOWING THAT MY
PROGRESS IS NOT BASED ON WHAT
OTHERS THINK IT SHOULD BE.

_____

_____

_____

_____

_____

_____

_____

_____

_____

_____

_____

I Take Courage in Knowing

Day 28

THE FACT THAT I GET A NEW DAY TO BE
MY BEST IS ENCOURAGEMENT IN ITSELF.

_____

_____

_____

_____

_____

_____

_____

_____

_____

_____

_____

_____

I Take Courage in Knowing

Day 29

I AM ENCOURAGED TO KNOW THAT MY PATH IS DESIGNED JUST FOR ME.

_____

_____

_____

_____

_____

_____

_____

_____

_____

_____

I Take Courage in Knowing

Day 30

I WILL TAKE COURAGE BECAUSE I
THOUGHT I WOULD NOT BE
HERE BUT I AM!

_____

_____

_____

_____

_____

_____

_____

_____

_____

_____

_____

I Take Courage in Knowing

Day 31

MY NEW FOUND COURAGE PUTS A SMILE ON MY HEART.

_____

_____

_____

_____

_____

_____

_____

_____

_____

_____

_____

Experience

Day 1

I WILL ALLOW MY EXPERIENCES
TO CONTINUE TO TEACH ME.

_____

_____

_____

_____

_____

_____

_____

_____

_____

_____

_____

Day 2

EVERYTHING I EXPERIENCE, WILL SHOW
ME SOMETHING NEW ABOUT MYSELF.

_____

_____

_____

_____

_____

_____

_____

_____

_____

_____

_____

_____

Day 3

EVERYTHING I GO THROUGH WILL
BUILD ME, AND NOT BREAK ME.

Day 4

I HAVE LEARNED THAT EVERYONE CAN NOT GO INTO MY FUTURE AND IT IS OKAY.

_____

_____

_____

_____

_____

_____

_____

_____

_____

_____

_____

_____

Day 5

I HAVE LEARNED THAT IT IS IMPORTANT TO PUT MYSELF FIRST.

_____

_____

_____

_____

_____

_____

_____

_____

_____

_____

Day 6

MY EXPERIENCES HAS TAUGHT ME
THAT I HAVE WHAT IT TAKES TO
ACHIEVE WHATEVER I PUT MY MIND TO.

_____

_____

_____

_____

_____

_____

_____

_____

_____

_____

_____

_____

Day 7

I HAVE LEARNED THAT EVERYTHING
DOES NOT HAVE TO HAPPEN AT ONCE.
SLOW AND STEADY WINS THE RACE.

_____

_____

_____

_____

_____

_____

_____

_____

_____

_____

_____

Day 8

CONTINUE WORKING TOWARDS THE
GOAL; YOU HAVE TO REMEMBER
WHY YOU STARTED.

_____

_____

_____

_____

_____

_____

_____

_____

_____

_____

_____

Day 9

I WILL LET GO OF THOSE THINGS THAT CAUSE ME TO BECOME ANXIOUS.

_____

_____

_____

_____

_____

_____

_____

_____

_____

_____

_____

Day 10

IN EXPERIENCE EVERYTHING IS
NOT EXPEDIENT; CONSISTENCY IS KEY.

_____

_____

_____

_____

_____

_____

_____

_____

_____

_____

Day 11

I WILL CONSISTENTLY BELIEVE IN MY
ABILITY, HAVING CONFIDENCE
IN WHO I AM.
THERE IS NO ONE LIKE ME.

Day 12

CELEBRATE YOUR ACCOMPLISHMENTS
IF NO ONE ELSE DOES. IT IS YOUR
JOURNEY, YOUR ACHIEVEMENTS.

_____

_____

_____

_____

_____

_____

_____

_____

_____

_____

_____

Day 13

IN EVERYTHING I DO, I WILL SEE
THE GOOD IN IT NO MATTER
THE OBSTACLES.

Day 14

MY EXPERIENCES HAVE TAUGHT ME
TO BE GRATEFUL WITH EVERY NEW
THING LEARNED; AND APPLY
IT TO MY DAILY ROUTINE.

Day 15

MY EXPERIENCES ARE TAILOR-MADE FOR ME; I WILL EMBRACE THEM.

_____

_____

_____

_____

_____

_____

_____

_____

_____

_____

_____

Experience

Day 16

I WILL WALK ONE DAY AT A TIME
AND EMBRACE MY NEWNESS.

_____

_____

_____

_____

_____

_____

_____

_____

_____

_____

_____

Day 17

MY EXPERIENCES HAVE SHOWN ME
HOW STRONG I AM, AND THAT I CAN
OVERCOME ANYTHING.

Day 18

I WILL LEARN TO ENCOURAGE MYSELF

_____

_____

_____

_____

_____

_____

_____

_____

_____

_____

_____

_____

Experience

Day 19

WHAT I LEARNED FROM MY EXPERIENCES I WILL SHARE TO ALL.

_____

_____

_____

_____

_____

_____

_____

_____

_____

_____

_____

Day 20

WHAT I HAVE BEEN THROUGH TAUGHT ME I AM STRONGER THAN I GIVE MYSELF CREDIT FOR.

_____

_____

_____

_____

_____

_____

_____

_____

_____

_____

Day 21

TAKE YOUR TIME AND EMBRACE YOUR
EXPERIENCE; THERE IS ALWAYS A
LESSON.

_____

_____

_____

_____

_____

_____

_____

_____

_____

_____

_____

Day 22

LET YOUR EXPERIENCE TEACH YOU
HOW TO BE DILIGENT AND PERSISTENT.

_____

_____

_____

_____

_____

_____

_____

_____

_____

_____

_____

Experience

Day 23

STAY CONSISTENT IN ALL YOU DO.
TAKE SELF EVALUATION.

_____

_____

_____

_____

_____

_____

_____

_____

_____

_____

_____

Day 24

REMEMBER YOU ARE NOT IN
COMPETITION WITH ANYONE BUT
YOURSELF. STRIVE TO BE BETTER
THAN THE DAY BEFORE.

Day 25

CELEBRATE EVERY ACCOMPLISHMENT
NO MATTER HOW LARGE OR SMALL.

_____

_____

_____

_____

_____

_____

_____

_____

_____

_____

_____

Day 26

EXPERIENCES TEACHES
YOU HOW TO BE ACCOUNTABLE.

_____

_____

_____

_____

_____

_____

_____

_____

_____

_____

_____

_____

Day 27

EXPERIENCE IS TEACHING ME THAT
THE OPINION OF OTHERS DOES NOT
DETERMINE MY SUCCESS.

_____

_____

_____

_____

_____

_____

_____

_____

_____

_____

_____

Day 28

LEARNING TO LIVE YOUR BEST LIFE EVERY DAY IS A GIFT.

_____

_____

_____

_____

_____

_____

_____

_____

_____

_____

_____

Day 29

EXPERIENCE WILL TEACH YOU
HOW TO WALK YOUR OWN PATH.

_____

_____

_____

_____

_____

_____

_____

_____

_____

_____

_____

_____

Day 30

BE GRATEFUL FOR EVERY EXPERIENCE
YOU GO THROUGH. IT DEVELOPS
CHARACTER.

Day 31

EVERYTHING YOU WENT THROUGH
HAS BUILT YOU STRONGER.

_____

_____

_____

_____

_____

_____

_____

_____

_____

_____

_____

_____

Growth

Growth

Day 1

GROWTH IS A DAILY PROCESS.

_____

_____

_____

_____

_____

_____

_____

_____

_____

_____

_____

Day 2

MY GROWTH PROCESS
IS A PERSONAL JOURNEY.

_____

_____

_____

_____

_____

_____

_____

_____

_____

_____

_____

Day 3

NOT STOPPING WHEN IT DIDN'T FEEL GOOD MADE ME STRONG.

_____

_____

_____

_____

_____

_____

_____

_____

_____

_____

_____

_____

Day 4

GROWING TAUGHT ME EVERYONE IS NOT APART OF MY DESTINY.

_____

_____

_____

_____

_____

_____

_____

_____

_____

_____

Day 5

CHOOSING ME IS NOT SELFISH,
IT IS SELF LOVE.

_____

_____

_____

_____

_____

_____

_____

_____

_____

_____

_____

Day 6

GROWING IS EVOLVING AND DEVELOPMENT.

_____

_____

_____

_____

_____

_____

_____

_____

_____

_____

_____

_____

Day 7

GROWTH DOES NOT HAPPEN OVER NIGHT; IT IS A PROCESS.

_____

_____

_____

_____

_____

_____

_____

_____

_____

_____

Day 8

GROWING MEANS KNOWING THAT
THINGS MAY CHANGE, BUT THE
PURPOSE IS THE SAME.

_____

_____

_____

_____

_____

_____

_____

_____

_____

_____

_____

Day 9

WHEN YOU BECOME OKAY WITH
SEPARATION FROM PEOPLE, YOU ARE
ON YOUR WAY TO DESTINY.

_____

_____

_____

_____

_____

_____

_____

_____

_____

_____

_____

Day 10

WHEN YOU CAN TRUST THE PLAN AND PROCESS THAT IS GROWTH.

Growth

Day 11

GROWING IS PUSHING THROUGH
DESPITE THE CHALLENGES.

Day 12

YOU ARE GROWING WHEN YOU DO
NOT NEED OTHERS TO CELEBRATE YOU.

Day 13

GROWTH IS NOT FOCUSING ON THE
NEGATIVE. HOWEVER, BEING
GRATEFUL FOR IT ALL.

_____

_____

_____

_____

_____

_____

_____

_____

_____

_____

_____

Day 14

GROWTH IS APPLYING WHAT YOU LEARNED ON A CONSISTENT BASIS.

_____

_____

_____

_____

_____

_____

_____

_____

_____

_____

Day 15

YOU HAVE TO KNOW YOUR ROAD
TO LEARNING. MATURITY IS YOURS
AND YOURS ALONE.

_____

_____

_____

_____

_____

_____

_____

_____

_____

_____

_____

Day 16

WHEN YOU EMBRACE CHANGE.
THAT'S GROWTH; KEEP EMBRACING.

_____

_____

_____

_____

_____

_____

_____

_____

_____

_____

_____

_____

Day 17

GOING THROUGH THE GROWING
PROCESS ULTIMATELY SHOW YOU HOW
MUCH YOU HAVE GROWN.

_____

_____

_____

_____

_____

_____

_____

_____

_____

_____

_____

_____

Day 18

GROWING MEANS BEING DETERMINED
WITH OR WITHOUT SUPPORT
FROM OTHERS.

_____

_____

_____

_____

_____

_____

_____

_____

_____

_____

_____

_____

Day 19

ONCE YOU HAVE GROWN, REACH BACK
AND HELP SOMEONE ELSE.

_____

_____

_____

_____

_____

_____

_____

_____

_____

_____

Day 20

I WILL ACKNOWLEDGE EVERYTHING
THAT MADE ME WHO I AM AT
THIS POINT IN MY LIFE.

_____

_____

_____

_____

_____

_____

_____

_____

_____

_____

_____

Day 21

GROWTH HAS TAUGHT AND
SHOWN ME MORE ABOUT MY SELF.

_____

_____

_____

_____

_____

_____

_____

_____

_____

_____

_____

Day 22

GROWTH GIVES YOU THE STRENGTH TO NEVER GIVE UP.

_____

_____

_____

_____

_____

_____

_____

_____

_____

_____

Day 23

GROWTH SAYS IT IS ME, I DETERMINE MY OUTCOME.

Day 24

I AM NOT IN COMPETITION WITH NO ONE. I AM COMPETING TO BE BETTER THAN I WAS THE DAY BEFORE.

_____

_____

_____

_____

_____

_____

_____

_____

_____

_____

Day 25

IT'S NOT ABOUT THE BIG THINGS,
IT IS ABOUT THE THINGS THAT
CAUSES CHANGE.

_____

_____

_____

_____

_____

_____

_____

_____

_____

_____

_____

Day 26

GROWTH TEACHES YOU
ACCOUNTABILITY NOT THE
BLAME GAME.

_____

_____

_____

_____

_____

_____

_____

_____

_____

_____

_____

Day 27

WHEN YOU ARE GROWING, THE
OPINIONS OF OTHERS HAVE
LESS VALUE.

_____

_____

_____

_____

_____

_____

_____

_____

_____

_____

_____

Day 28

IN THE GROWTH PROCESS PRIORITIES
BECOME CLEAR AND IMPORTANT.

_____

_____

_____

_____

_____

_____

_____

_____

_____

_____

_____

Day 29

KEEPING YOUR DETERMINATION,
THE OBSTACLES ARE TRUE
SIGNS OF GROWTH.

_____

_____

_____

_____

_____

_____

_____

_____

_____

_____

Day 30

GROWTH IS DETERMINED BY
INDIVIDUAL ACCOMPLISHMENTS.

_____

_____

_____

_____

_____

_____

_____

_____

_____

_____

_____

Day 31

LOOKING AT WHERE I WAS COMPARED
TO WHERE I AM, I AM PROUD OF
MYSELF.

_____

_____

_____

_____

_____

_____

_____

_____

_____

_____

_____

_____

With All My Broken Pieces God Made Me Whole

Made in the USA
Columbia, SC
06 September 2025

61962001R00091